HURON COUNTY LIBRARY

O9-BRZ-509

HURON COUNTY LIB

3 6492 00471160 9

819.154 Clark

Clark, H.
The dwelling of weather.

PRICE: $15.00 (3559/ex   )

THE DWELLING OF WEATHER

Hilary Clark

THE DWELLING OF WEATHER

Brick Books

SEP 1 6 2003

National Library of Canada Cataloguing in Publication

Clark, Hilary Anne, 1955-
    The dwelling of weather / Hilary Clark.

Poems.
ISBN 1-894078-26-8

    I. Title.

PS8555.L363D94 2003   C811'.54   C2003-900368-X
PR9199.3.C5224D94 2003

Copyright© Hilary Clark, 2003

We gratefully acknowledge the Canada Council for the Arts,
the Government of Canada through the Book Publishing Industr
Development Program (BPIDP), the Ontario Arts Council, and
the Saskatchewan Arts Board for supporting the publication of
this book.

The painting on the cover is by Greg Hardy, "Day in August",
2001, acrylic on canvas, 56 in. x 90 in.
The author's photograph was taken by Cindy Moleski.

This book is set in Sabon.
Design and layout by Alan Siu.
Printed and bound by Sunville Printco Inc.

Brick Books
431 Boler Road, Box 20081
London, Ontario N6K 4G6

brick.books@sympatico.ca

For my children —
Julian, Nina,
& Evan

TABLE OF CONTENTS

4

Notes

Acknowledgements

Life Stories

*The shadow past is shaped by
everything that never happened.
Invisible, it melts the present like
rain...*

Anne Michaels, *Fugitive Pieces*

1

That face— it shines, shriven in a rain
beyond water.

Fauré's *Requiem*, mud and wine—
a child's nest of foolish eggs.

All I know is what I see
near-sightedly—
        I hardly recall this life
hallowed as it is with grief,
invisibility—

My days are given to shadows,
nights to other suns— lives
in paint-box colours

        an unlived, real as rain.

প্র

Slim feet in the desert— leaves spring
from each step.

What is knowing but snow
veiling the sun?
                I have no eyes, the old
black carrion has claimed me.

Corridors, a house of storms.
                The past swims up,
swims away.

Mozart sings the dead.
I dream of rooms so empty
they vanish—
                my head filled with winds
and choirs.

Yet rain, the greens and sepias
of spring.

Bel canto for the resurrection,
songs for the unlived
                    fading

Split to bitter sap—
intuition—
            snow geese, a black-tipped wind

Ravens play on the updraft,
glide—
            I aspire to that lightness

Gulls call from the clouds
and fall
            tense—

spring's waters
                breaking—

2

When day turns its amber face
to the mirror—
          flies, sticky wings—

When shadows fly from my startled mouth
and I have no nets, no lines
to hold them—

Another life?
                    as likely
as this August moon— full, doubled
in the glass
          green moths
glistening in stove light—

                         as likely
as these sudden bruises, crow's feet,
swoons—

Another body rises, brittle sheath—
                    locusts spit in the fire—

                    ❧

Tawny beads, thread-snapped—
the hours rattle in a bag.

Along autumn avenues, the elms
drop lace handkerchiefs
on our faces.

Each moment over-ripe with another,
another
        the long bough drooping
                        to spill—

This is the hollow of love
and fear
        lunar flowers dapple the body
        — silver, white—

assumption, a woman
folded into bliss—

a year of scattered selves
                pink pigeons, blurred wings—

                ❧

Hours on fire, cat's fur
sparks to touch.

Here we are facing west,
spring's explosives at our backs
                    we fly—

Just now I held a globe
of rain— tempest
in a crystal—

a moment's white fold
a crumpled cone of freesias.

Our minds clear
as we climb
                no footholds
for fear—

praising, falling

lifted like kittens,
squalling—

The First Day

A day on the path, you gather your robes about you
      — blue, of twisted wind, a spring's anguish—
of cold wind, blue bruised to violet,
your new feet bleeding

      your life at your lips, numb, bitter—
torn morsels of bread.

A road of scrub and blowing sage, cloud-scraps
      you are approaching
a hole in your memory, your breath
sucked through—

      don't touch me

a past of milk and fire
just formed

      no, *don't*
touch

It is always thus—
the approach, clouds quickening

      holes, sudden holes—
a rim of sparkling water, a life
flows through

      I will be with you
always
      all your questions
failing—

❧

First light—
each day a breaking, boulder
rolled away
                    the night flies out—
bats, faceless birds

— hold me, I'm afraid
to dream again.

The face shone like lightning—
tidings of earthquakes
girding the earth
        women singing inside the sun.

He is not where you look
on the myrrh-scented stone
but elsewhere—
        hungry, cold

Lilies, an alien lacquer of blood
        thin feet

intimations—

ॐ

Struggling to rise—
drugged with oil and spice,
held back—
            tatters of flesh, linen,
earthly clutter
                    hunger

Do not bring your hands,
narrow, unlined

            do not bring your lips—

no, turn away from the gaping door
            the door we fear and covet— rising,
held only by the arm, sleep-heavy,
thrown over us.

Morning wears a white robe—
                    apple-blossoms, ecstasies
of bees and robins, sleeping cats—
            it's warm, here are messages
tucked in the earth
                    he is not here
not here, laugh the magpies

        here, echo the crows

as we wake in the rags
        of our vision.

                    ✑

Touch me—
      no ghost has flesh
as I have.

On the first day, first dawn—
      nested leaves, a rustling

a breeze, warm breath
      receive me—

we stir, we stir
      touch me,
no ghost

    only the past,
fine hairs lifting

    the return of hope,
whose wounds

    always new—

Nine Wilds

> *…That your white bones may arise,*
> *And your limbs be joined anew.*
>
> Chang Heng, "The Bones of Chuang Tzu"

1

A day of bones, floating ash,
new snow. Such pain—

I walk into fear and thickening cloud.
A day of white eyes,

the dead waiting. From west to east
to zones beyond naming—

each organ in its throne
each absent throat screaming.

2

Having crossed the Nine Wilds,
followed by a moon as close
as your pained and dreaming face—

having hidden in abandoned airports,
the luggage arriving empty—

having swallowed the last grains,
staring at the winking clock,

a ticket dropped, a coin, a pin—
no lesson.

Only bones, the long, moaning desolation
of the coast.

To the Bonehouse

And geese fly over the dark river,
crying *I, I*—
   in a crown of leaves,
blighted, coppery—

I would open a new door,
a last door
   the squares of the city wintry,
lacking signs—
     tongue in a knot,
all my lines kicked away—

I would follow a life of want,
emptying,
an autumn of moons
     heavy, huge
with hours.

I would go with the black robes
down to the bonehouse—
   lie down without amulets,
poems
   only ivory, whalebone
     moon-fingered vertebrae

cadavre exquis— whose longing
sleep—

Nature morte

Red grapes, the bloom of flesh,
of tongues.
                    Compose a life
of fallen things—
petals, blue corolla
of the heart.

Nature morte.
                    All that we love
escapes us, lilac on humid air.

Larvae, rapt, shroud the leaves
of summer—
                    our knowing
                                        hangs
on slim threads.

Place the vase upon the sill.
Tiger lily, bluest aster,
eye of sun—
                    all water, lovely
curving form.

*Still life with flowers
in an olive jar.* Seek nothing
beyond the dying—
                    a few brown leaves,
anemones like babies' faces—

the painter's trembling hand.

Other Worlds

London, England

Shadows in the inner parlour, Alice skittering with a kitten.
The skein of wool unwinds, pink-flecked, knotted. Here
in the city, new leaves and bud-sockets bursting with
little pangs of bliss. Cold wind, ducks ruffle their curls.
The odd hen pecks for grace. Roosters echo over Russell
Square, traffic rumbles in answer. Perhaps a black taxi,
a whisper, a coin. You'd be gone, no-one would have
known you.

So transient, chalk marks on wet stone. The grey rains
pour and pour— nothing left, only small whimsies of
style, red umbrellas. Quiet jazz caught on the radio's
edge, a car accelerating into the night. In another hour,
the novel will end. You read on— each word could be
others, thresholds to possible tales. Forsythia on a rising
breeze, yellow petals   briefly

Under your eyelids the sky is red. Puddles on the street, broken stone. Foreign tongues, the corners of your mouth are bleeding. A child casts an ancient shadow. The trees hang upside down, the daffs are foolish clarions. A daily armageddon of trucks and drills, manholes open— one blast, another, a ghostly baseline following.

The bow drawn out so slow. Violet, fuchsia, blue— jewelled dresses lean into the music. A thousand watching eyes. A sheet of music falls, and you are walking west along the Thames. You are walking east, your footsteps leave no imprint. Spikes of green, there's the nub, now pushing into the sun. A woman's face in a basement window— a small room with armchairs, just so. You have begun your descent into the earth.

The way is negative, light and dark reverse. Who is that ghost in the video monitors, turning toward the door. Spring bleeds through crocuses, saffron cups. A purple Lent. The stations of a life are few but endlessly repeated: shoulder, stumble, yield. Old women pause on each corner, insubstantial. Every hour with its shadow. The young laugh and eat and lick their fingers. They link arms, but you pass through.

Even the yellow primula ghosts its own possibilities. You scrape the mud off your shoes and go in, crying. Whose is that face behind the whistling kettle? In another life, you would know. Rain beats on the kitchen window. The knowledge can't be written, not legibly anyway. And the daffodils would be blue in those gardens (here large, immodest as the sun). Tomorrow you will gather your poems, fold them into swans and float them down the river, vanishing.

Melancholy

A box tied with night ribbons—
Andromeda, Coma
                    Cassiopeia   faintly

A melancholy box tied with rain—
            ink-stained catalogues of clouds
nephologists lost in fog

And tied with waterfalls, vines
            a box of macaws,
macaques

            tied with infant hair, purses
of shrunken years—
            of amethysts, coral, pearls,
baby teeth.

With age, a mind drops
its bundles—
                moons, engrams—
maps of every library, catalogues,
books—

        bundles of postcards, epigraphs,
final words— sonnets, comics,
comedies, boys' stories,
locked diaries—
                tempests, wutherings
    hauntings

        and page by burning page
a book of common prayer,
dark psalms

to a darker author.

Book of Spleen

1

This is a book of melancholy,
read it through one white night or

slowly, in long rain, in afternoons
dripping hour by hour.

This is a book of sleep.
Whisper again of that far horn

heard, the flute's elliptical drift.
This is a book of dying,

a pillow book stuffed with owl feathers,
snow. I will read as far as the woods go.

The path vanishes behind me.

❧

The book of salacity falls open on spring—
pussy willow, virgin's bower,

gloved fingers twisting each tender flower.
Flurries of white confetti, mock-orange—

all illusion, even to the last tear.
I am admiring your body,

its long limbs and spasms, I am reading
a book of Zen gardens,

ten black robes swaying on a line.
On the scale from opal to light,

a child's milk teeth disappear.
Bring in the relics, the glass ones,

your mother's frail ankle bones, wrists.
Pull down the book of ghostly law,

scan its endless lists, its burgeoning vines
of last words, first words,

tenets for the quick and the dead.
I'm done with writing, its trickery—

obscurity at noon, cold clarity
at midnight— I'm done

with vicarious lines. The best life
is shut in a book.

2

What shadows read us tales
in bed— ladybirds, mermaids, spiders,

curds and whey, blackberries and cream,
chamomile for naughty bunnies.

Through what rooms, what pages are we led—
our precious books shed leaves,
unbind, lost aerogrammes

fly home. Where can *we* fly,
our bodies heavy with cloud and snow?

The kettle whistles—

there's a message in your tea,
the black dregs clinging to your cup.

Read the old meandering lists, catalogues
of frost stars, trilobites,

verse forms, pythons, the phases
of Phobos, shrouds of the moon.

Take up and read
this book of spleen and silence,

sidelong words.
Yeats' paradisal birds,

A Child's Garden of Verse—
dust—

3

The years turn one way, one way—
A winter system, vanes spinning north,

spires and empty squares, loose balconies,
even the boldest chickadees

stunned—
that rose, ice pink, in your lapel.

The years make strange wedding guests,
telling no stories, only

litanies of wind and lust,
pages licked and held to the light.

Oh come and dance, deliver me
from these never-ending inky poems,

reams of musty paper—

mushrooms in the dark, that tang
of fungus, urine, rain.

Will it clear— the weather—
one snowdrop, green—

Woman Reading 1

little/ memory jars//empty of their pickled plums
Michael Palmer, "On the Way to Language"

Memory jars— where was
that phrase—
        a book of poems turned over,
its faint marginalia fading,
as sleep. . .
        a woman reading
yawns, the phrase taken
into the earth.

        She dreams
of stone jars, urns
of precious words, jars
that will shatter if she turns
to look—
        the inscriptions too faint,
or foreign— Aramaic? Greek?
what trace remains,
the jars empty of wine, the guests
having fled—
                only clay and ash,
mummified wasps, two flies
buzzing the rim—

                    She dreams
she is tracing the elusive phrase
through a library—
                    memory jars
on every page,
on spines maroon or green,
            gilt lettering—
                    voilà, the very phrase
pulled out of pockets, inkpots,
top hats, sleeves
                    the odd moth too
and *memory* flutters from her ear
to the last, highest book—
                            escapes

as she wakes.

Woman Reading 2

She holds a blue letter. Some tale of forbidden love? Sunlight through the open window, her knees warm with it, parting— *sshh*, two older sisters in the doorway. They have learned to wait, to gaze at the wallpaper flowers (a border of clove pinks) until their eyes fail and they vanish. The sea, her bliss, rushes in.

Moroccan cushions, purple and rust, a white sheet spotted with blood. She leans over the letter, its bouquets of parting words— *plum, nipple, silk*. Two sidelong sisters enter bearing tea. She is reading slowly the garden of her body, wallpaper pinks round her head. Virgin buds and musky blossoms. Mirrors fold the room into light.

Something in this picture flees, a word. A woman's bodice trembling with roses (pinks on the wall), hand reaching for a teacup. Two sisters on the slant of a question. Scattered papers, French novels. Reading, she tastes sugar on her lips. Sunny palm fronds in a jar, mirrors reflecting sea.

The tale ends with a cry, a cascade of blue paper. Roses, shattered china. A woman's face among flowers, fallen cushions. Two sisters in the doorway, two upright backs. Black silk. They have learned to wait, to read with the utmost discretion. Soon they will leave the picture, mirrors hollowed out in the dusk.

Woman in a Striped Dress

Black chrysanthemums. A woman muses, inclined,
petals falling. Her mind is a dim room papered with
roses, lamps turned low, a faint gold nimbus. A doll
or familiar hovers in a corner— *Mama, look at me.*
But she is a woman oblivious among flowers, iris,
dying ferns. An auburn-haired woman dressed in rust
and cream, arranging the hours: stems and foliage,
spidery fronds, one scarlet star punctuating the dead.
Here a box of black ribbons, an indolent elbow. The
woman beside her is a sombre leaf in the pattern. The
child in the corner looks away. And we turn in silence
also, bearing black chrysanthemums, the woman,
within us.

Broken

A woman's trace, trick ghosts in the blood. The brain
is a rank garden overgrown with swollen pods. Our
chameleon lusts— cobalt nipples, scarlet throat, breath
inconstant as fire. In a rhythm of hiccups, a woman
rises between the sheets. Even in sackcloth the sex insists.
A basket of rowan berries, cloves.

Ashes drift, first snowflakes on your sleeve. Ice-clouds
bury the river, soon all the thermometers will freeze. In
a flame of light, the other passes through
                    you broken, waiting with empty arms—

Digression

*But I am wandering off into irrational
magnitudes. . .*
Susan Howe, "Pythagorean Silence"

1

New moon, the dark in your face
blots the stars

but I digress— stepping off the edge, the long
sinuous edge of loss—

from a story of hauntings,
unlived lives

invisible threads from leaf to leaf—
the spider's silent tact—

white pebbles on the trail. I dwell
in a garden of syllables

take up and read

willow in my eye

alloy of lead & gold
        a magpie's nest of rags,
ephemera—

2

When the flood sweeps our minds
into alien forms—
                minnow, raven,
jonquil in a breeze

when we put on our garments
of aspen
                flax bending blue,
white islands

when we read the sun & planets
on tattered cards—
                our deaths
pinned, fluttering, along the sky

we slip into another order
(reticence, whispers).

Listen—
                stallions thunder
in the godless clouds

our fettered feet
                stumble

No path— no beacons, fires—
                just wheat and dipping

constellations.

Weather Notes: St. Peter's Abbey

Weather is memory every time.
Fred Wah,"Father/Mother Haibun #3"

June 26

    A weather shift, each sky particular yet overlaid with other possibilities. The air is dense with moods. Rain streaks the window but my eyes are clear. Today, I touched the hem of a higher design: matte white with tucks and dimples, longer folds, silver, over the treetops. Migraine's sheaf of prickly leaves. Rising wind and magpie screams, the human reduced to a few elements— footsteps, engine, muddy slap of tires—

                  Look, yellow leaves already. Imagine what you will, the sky is empty. Farm machines in the dark, the mind also. Cold puts a finger on the air, the slightest pressure; messages run like mice along the wires. The eyes' strict discipline. But even in pain, with eyes squeezed shut, I can sense the sky clearing, wind shaking green from the trees. On the last day the crows will croak *ave*, we will awaken to magpies, winnowing wings.

June 27

Slow Sabbath prayers, fluff drifts from cottonwoods. Hollows, handfuls of cloud. Owl eyebrows. Tufts and shapeless things— how draw the line? Description with a cloud finger, self-effacing. *Very like a whale*, a cup, a moustache. The gods frown and gape, dissolving into water drops. Words I have written, words I haven't— deleted. Magpies retch and puke, and mirrors break. Crows comprehend, *ah, ah*. And grace? The clouds are stacked mosquito-screens, obstacles to the light. Cloud hay bales, cotton balls, commas. Rain swells the sky. I am quilting a pillow, grey-blue and pearl. I am making this up, alas, inky feathers in the dust.

June 28

A cursor crosses the computer screen, a fly head-butts the window. Summer enters my cell. Shadows on the keys, yellow leaves. The mind embarks on colours— yellow brown, nut brown, dust brown, taupe. Lilacs in the garden, creamy pink; green in the bottle-glass chapel. Aspen, dandelion wind— the universe swarms with mosquitoes. Who am I in this insect infinity of grass and dry leaves falling? Mary is in her ants' nest, praying. Mary is in her frail gazebo, murmuring psalms of praise. Ants and termites bear the cross away. Pick up your pen and follow me—

how easily the world vanishes into the poem. A small grey cloud means rain: "Oh dear," sighs Bear, holding a blue balloon, floating up, a string of cloudlets behind him. I would change my mind as a cloud changes, leaving tails of vapour. Spiders drop from the heavens, their lacquered red backs inscribed with cryptic messages: *No Scotch. Void. Empty.*

June 30

There's an opening in mind, blue keyhole the crows fly through. Oviduct. Arrowhead. White beard. An old man bends in the vegetable patch, weeding among onions, orange poppies. Succulent song, a robin. Up there a wrist, a teacup of cloud. Our words are not fit for use, wool toques pulled over our eyes. Clouds like brains, brains like clouds— ridges and fjords, inner inlets. Snow synapses, the weather napping, fitful. The most beautiful lake is on the other side of the mountain; discovered, it shrinks to a tear. We flee, overtaken by shadow bears, great grey rags. Dust the book, open it, and let your finger fall: *prism*. The sun burns your eyes, and you see.

July 1

Mouth to mouth, little morsels of flesh. A woodpecker taps time beyond the scrapping of ravenous babies. The lilies drain of colour. Leaf pebble. Eyebrow twig. Fluff suspended from a spider's thread. Dry leaf, *tap*— my hat. This papery heart's on the point of tearing away. Thoughts fly off, one after another. Spruce tops creak, invisible printers. Strains of O *Canada*, the ants pause on their looping paths—

begin again. White-robed Mary, pray for us, for the wounded and vulnerable lacking legs and antennae, for the killers with hard berry hearts. A garden of imminent apples. A woman's body swells and swells, watermelon belly. Babies fuss at the beak, demanding black pap. Cloud-teats oozing ice cream: sky-blue migraine. In the intervals between squawks, thinking at the speed of light. Winged integers disappear into the sun.

July 4

How many words for shadow? *Ombre, ombra,*
Schatten. Tenebrae, sun's dying. A day of fumbling, of
half-glimpsed pattern— dregs in my coffee cup, fingers
finding the keys. The magpie gang's left town, other
birds move in, swiftly. Robin on a wire; robin with
worm; robin plummeting to earth with suave aplomb.
Russet sparrows with brains of bread. A large monarch
mimics a finch, yellow leaf. A crow echoes its own caw,
ironic.

Wait, the bell— one. Unseen machines stop,
silence filling the intervals. Those damn magpies back
too soon, arguing, hanging out their rags. Plunder strung
from branch to branch, pockets turned out. My
thoughts are spiked and crossed with brittle branches.
Children's cries in the distance. Crows would perch
on my grandmother's deodar, making nests of her long
grey hair. That tapping again— fingernails, wood
cracking? A garden of days sliding one over another,
slate over blue, breeze over song

sparrows in their spheres of green light

July 6

A veil falls between eye and lilac. The red emergency ladder offers no escape. Now a week has passed, the lilacs are brown shadows of their former selves. Yellow leaves on the grass, out of season. How will I die? Under a lilac tree, that scent sealing the end? Too much wind, the clouds move too quickly, streaming like thoughts on an extra half-tab a day— *nervy*— tents, castles, islands setting sail. A white face appears over the trees, becomes a prehistoric fish, smudged mushroom with delicate stipe. Clouds can be anything the childish eye desires: elephants, pandas, zoo parades. A monk on a tricycle, carrying trash. Celestial lawn mowers— at times I lose my thinking rhythm, its small bird intervals. A robin watches me, cocking his head. When I die, what will I see? My own beaked face looking back at me.

July 7

Winged insects, neurons in their random firing. A white sky antsy with rain. The grass has grown long in the hedged enclosure. Light flickers through the elms. Excess, excess, sex in the *Star-Phoenix*. A tiny red bug, flick, a green smear. Killer humidity in the East, but here a cool haze, morning veil. Soon all will fall according to the season. The magpies have moved on again, their absence audible. *Where are you going?* someone shouts. Who knows? Can a balance be found between destination and ravishing drift?

Dandelions in the grass, wild succulents. A woman weeds among rhubarb, stems jewel-red, sour-sweet.

Weather Body

1

Open any window, the sea blows in. In the middle of
Saskatchewan, in a gale, flags snapping. I know nothing—
the weather is the ground of my understanding, it blows
and moans incessantly. The unlived is a wind stinging the
ears, jostling, gnawing at our doors. Rain opens the mailbox,
chuckles in the gutters. In another life I am transparent
and the weather an ink-blue stain. Names I cannot
remember chirp in the winter lilac. *Me, me, me*, the one
the cat brought in.

Winter smoke. Sunrise red and sailors' warning. I read the
Odyssey and then, between the lines, I unread. Odysseus
returns to his mistress's bed, Penelope winds up her silk.
Just a feather, sere leaf— a life's reverse measure.

❧

In this net of invisible knots, nothing. *Nil, nil, nil.* Your
hair is strung with water-beads, scarlet berries. Tiptoe up
the muddy lane, past guard dogs and compost heaps, gates
gaping open as you pass. Go as far as the leaning hut. The
mist is thickening, shrouding the hermit who sleeps within.

A small boy offers a nest. Fluff and twigs, open to all winds.
The rain it raineth every day, our bodies vulnerable, perfect.

2

Could I admit the light, salt-prism'd, dazzling— *Now, very now,* I apprehend: the old crow's opening its wings. The unlived is a shiver of leaves, the weather sighing in our ears. Low intimations of ocean. These are my books, whose starred, wavy pages— spells— speculative inner leaves—

Ice storms blow out of the north. I know enough to hide in a house of books, pressing my ear to the wall— lovers softly moaning, pilgrims marking their stations. I know enough to dissimulate, a thing of moss and silence.

☙

We move in a mesh of glass. Nets glisten, the sea... we forget. A fevered sun, a mouldy orange. Smells of decay haunt our dwellings. Worms lie curled in private vaults; dying, we invade their sleep. Whose face, whose features emerging?

When I was a child, I gathered eggs: purple, yellow, and blue. I laid my years in a wicker basket, no one told me how fragile—

broken—

Summer Doors

Cypress Hills

1

In this breakfast light, a threshold—
knife-cut sill, guillotine
shadow
        tendrils of ivy, wisteria
remembered.

I have tried to enter, beating on a door
that is always open
                turning away,
failure burned into my palms.

Walls of warm stone,
shadow
        poppy breeze
I sleep and write—
            startle, fall
when I come too close

           the threshold
changing with each breath—
its keen edge
        now indefinite, I am
too drowsy to see.

Lay it down and dwell
in a house that adds rooms
          as a bubble adds hemispheres
with each breath—
                    iridescent, glimpsed
above treetops—

          light into mind

mind into trembling
                    form

2

Among lodgepoles—
       looking up, one ear to the wind,
incipient storm—
              pssssst—
sing the pine cones to the fire

Thinking conflagrations
       startled by falling branch
and animal scent, my fears—

       the bear that is not here,
the mother moose that is—

       mosquitoes ravish me—

clouds and firebreaks, blackened wood.

Imagine the flames in their desire leaping, leaping
to cross—

       trees like those long, ornamental matchsticks,
struck— flaring turquoise, jade—

       the child coveting that fire—

Deadfalls, red needles underfoot
         the air sighing *seee,*
the aspen's moving face

       I would be mended

but am torn, mind
       from leaf—

3

Pinetops bow as I write—
        slow breathing, morning—

write to recover from the dream's humiliations
                passport, purse and coat— all lost,
the woman flayed in her nakedness,
fleeing—

The forest is fingering rain
        blue spruce, pines

white-tails
        vanishing.
Dense sleep— a forest's
thickening mist

                that bird—
red-winged blackbird
        preening, opening its beak

its liquid call
        spilling

                and the woman walks beneath it
wearing too many layers of clothes—
naming
        cow parsley, old-man's-beard

a wind stirs the names
        splash of hail

sunlight on the hillside, passing shadow.

Dwelling: Prologue

The house has grown into mind—
empty, draped with Spanish moss.
Leaning in, I can almost
taste them—
                rooms filling with sea,
with long amnesic strands of kelp.
                Her grey hair twists
around my fingers— pin pricks,
drowsy recognitions.

Ghosts in a house sliding into the sea.
Last night, I dreamed of running home—
all the way to the coast, yes
                the last lights strung along the mountains—
but the way was blocked, the meaning
lost to me
                hard arms pinning me back.

Breathe the scent of woodchips, tar
and enter a poem where cedar fires burn,
night moths flinging themselves   home

A child's tree house, green residue of weathers.
Rooms folded within rooms—
                dogwood, bottle glass,
showers of rain— paper gulls
on a mobile
          turning.

A poem is a shelter,
provisional— a little wobbly—

a house whose rooms have no walls,
whose windows are prairie sloughs
            whose ceilings stream
                        with the clouds.

I want to ride my bicycle through
your house and riding,
dwell there—
            I want to slip through—

In my father's house are many rooms—
lined with dim jars
                crabapples, pink
moons, dills in bitter weeds—

such airs in the night!
                Flutes, funereal
horns, I wake to mourn
my own passing.

I may slam all the doors, run away—
the house encompasses me.

I haven't gone out much lately.
A shadow moves from room to room.

My poems get misplaced, so I keep them
in my head—
   my head hurts
with their singing.

Dwelling

On hot afternoons I have built houses of dust motes, houses that dissemble, shift with each breath. Lily ponds, irises— my moods turn upon a carp's whim. The house may rise, windows flashing in the sun. The house may fall, muddy, brushed by fins.

❧

Take care, thresholds are deceptive. Lured by the promise of sugar, a child has disappeared. There's a door somewhere behind those brambles, those fat berries that stain teeth black. Light on our backs and shadow on our faces.

❧

Knock, and it shall be opened. The door of the house that has never been fades when we approach it. We can only imagine the cool vestibule, the hand extended toward us. Yet we walk through the rooms already, rooms lined with urns of lilies, shelves of uncut books— *The Tempest, Song of Songs, Mother Goose.* The right light will open them.

❧

Pass through the door and through the walls, summer bricks warm to the skin. Scent of pines; distant, droning planes. This is the house of your earliest waking. A dwarf cottage grown over with hollyhocks. A witch's sugared bait. Mice and hedgehogs, rabbits and ducks— infant worlds, permeable. A door painted blue and crossed by clouds.

A stray phrase entering this vestibule can efface it: *white as new lambswool; folded, a rose.* Metaphors try as they may. New cows moo in your ears. Longing has built this vestibule; longing will tear it down. And build again, from spidery blueprints.

Pine-figures bring sleep to sleep. You doze in brief intervals, half-awake on the sunny bed. The unlived returns in reading, between ink-printed lines. Alice steps through her image, a kitten becomes a queen. A small girl wakes in a hole in a tree, and it's home forever after— maple spinners, pine cones, smell of pitch on sticky fingers. Pages turn, and Alice half-drowns in a sea of tears.

Vespers in the next valley, but here a deepening silence. With each year a notebook is opened and shut, title on the spine just legible. *Cumulus. Willow. Thunderhead. Sage.* And the spaces between, unwritten.

Unlit corridors, empty rooms— a house of silence rises stone by stone. When you speak, the house echoes. Crying out, you feel foundations shifting. Hush, little baby— go back to the first room, warm as milk. A room with soft walls you press a cheek against, sleepy, walls lightly freckled and scented.

Hunger and the passing hours. The first room no more than an alcove of flesh, a hollow in a crooning world. A nightingale's passion in every tree, garden walls tangled with pinks and honeysuckle. What clouds in the sky, what characters, fading?

The first room lines every room you have slept in, orienting its windows, polishing their panes. As if, waking, another scene might appear, another face in the morning glass. Are you here? A knife of light divides the air.

Curled in bed or in the grass— the heat too much, the years, the heavy, dogged years— you dream a room, silent, cool, your tears drying, heart's lurching motion stilled. Briefly. The plaque on the wall reading "Love me."

᷂

Freesias for sickness, nostalgia's excess. Leaves of shadow on the wall. Between each phrase, a ruined garden— morning glory, moss, massed brambles.

In mind, an iris with its purple shadow. The dark throat of longing, too dark to touch. Draw down the blind and open a book of gardens (cultivated, hedged with weapons). All your art is an edgy return, a veering off down paths of flattened grass. Peregrinations, circling home.

You build your house with whatever is at hand. On this August day, the prairie swallows its tiny farms. Fearing fire, muffled thunder. One raindrop, just—

a door opening in the wall of heat—

&

The house contains all the houses you have ever lived in— rooms forgotten, childish things. A house of creased pages, settling into fiction. White shingles in the sun, vine maples, a single photo remains. A child's tree house, an alcove under the deodar. You no longer distinguish between memory and speculation, mind porous, the world open to suggestion.

Mysteries, ghost stories, tales of war. Crosswords already pencilled in. As children we built up trembling towers of dominoes, card houses, and fought to knock them down. Then built again, following some inner necessity. One room opens onto another, then another, and they're all lined with books, they *are* the book, its sentences. A story of doorways and thresholds, hidden drops. What footfall in the hall—

you wake in the dark, disoriented, heart pounding. Return to the boy tracing sand with a stick. Something retreats under a rock or hunkers down in a clam hole; small lakes quake underfoot. Return to the girl shaping nests among huckleberries, forts in the forest to read in. The past returns, but in the key of *might have been*, the minor key of the unlived.

❧

Here is a honeycomb of rooms, cells for contemplation.
The ways in are beyond number— one hovers, unable to
decide. Is this the way the mind dies, facing so many
thresholds it swoons?

The night is a castle of stars— dark ramparts, precipitous
stairways. One can decipher the emblems or ink in new
constellations: the Black Flag, the Snake, with Amoeba at
the periphery, its syllables floating, touching, contracting.
Migraine antennae. You climb the hill to the top and open
the first door, sage scent fading, wind falling still. There's
a bed in here, an invisible sleeper bunching up the sheets,
lightly snoring. You slide in, open the *Purgatorio*, and
begin to read.

In the middle years, when the music must be recomposed
each morning; when all sequence is broken, when small
doors slam shut in the poem; when the house is too small,
and the garden firmly gated— what is it to begin again?
The elms drop their leaves in the dark.

❦

Guitar along cool corridors. Enter a room of lacquered
rosewood, walls knocking softly as you walk. A music
measured along the nerve, sinews, fingers thinking.
Bach's transparent rooms. The right fingers are sore,
the left barely stretch to the chords. Flesh scored,
remembering.

Put your ear along the stone— a hidden room? On the
other side, something hushes. Smell of cedar, fern. The
forest closes behind you, words flitting, whistling from
their perches.

The end of the passage cannot be foreseen. Each room
is a garden promising a virginal memory— white irises,
perhaps, or a fountain of silver coins. The eye a window,
opening. Ferns fringe the sun. The hinge is attention
to the moment, its particular light. A lattice, fine
lacework; the retina draws its veil.

෨

In the house of equivocation, courtyards outnumber rooms. Here it is always evening, ceilings rolling, heavy with rain. Gardens of turbulent verbs, violet flourishes— all lush, all mossy, phrasal, one path appended to another, then another. Fountains of lives, half-spilled.

In the house of dreams, rooms shift their furniture as you sleep. A mirror winks from the floor, a blue carpet lids the window. Waking each day, you are lost and must begin anew. Place freesias in one room, a cat licking its toes. Place a girl's long lashes, wet lilacs, a rose. Commit these images to mind, tomorrow they'll be shuffled, transformed: a girl with freesia eyes, a cat with lilac whiskers. A rose for your thoughts.

In the house of the unlived, the rooms have no walls, no ceilings. Our walking feet measure tentative dimensions. Swallows fly home to invisible eaves. The air is wet and cool, the clouds golden colanders. Rain, rain— are we tasting our tears? Will oceans flood the corridors, the cellars of sleeping children? Killer whales surface, swim among us.

❧

Lord, I have dreams. Swept weeping in waters, the corridors rushing water, arteries turbulent, opening. Fringes of flesh, clear eels. *La noyée*, hair streaming, fingers of seaweed, anemone. In the house of memory, bodies are porous. We wash and rinse and squeeze moments through.

Dreams of water, the flood lapping the upper windows. A baby laughs among the screams. You climb to the attic to watch the flotillas of paper lifeboats. The walls are holding, just. If they burst— the library breaking open, books on the back of the flood, books with wavy water-logged leaves. Books of ice-treks to the poles, journeys to the bottom of the sea. Books of Mother Goose and lullabies, herbs and secret spells of love. Of optics and the properties of crystal, and why minds shatter as they do. Through the upper windows— holding, just— you look into jade alcoves, courtyards. Memory.

A room is floating on the surface of the sea. In a trick of perspective, Gulliver's snug box is suddenly huge, and is hauled on board to the wonder of all. A room is carried on the swell, toy table and chairs sliding this way, that way, miniscule portraits tilting. A room of glass fills with water, sinking through its own green reflection.

ᦁ

Past lights, a dwelling in loss and possibility. The prairie slough catches, reflects you, thought streaming, assuming transient forms overhead. A brief excursion has become a journey— no return, doors shutting quietly behind you, the path through the long grass buzzing with insects.

August light, the piper's tune is clear water. The children emerge from memory. Come with me, he plays, to a dwelling without dimension, without adults or tears. Where it is always morning, where crippled limbs melt away for desire. Where pears and apples scent the corridors and breezes carry melody. Come with me.

A dream of a child drawn up from a well. He is dead, he is only sleeping, cheeks still pink. All these years you have been preparing a room for him— a narrow bed, white sheets, flowering hawthorn through the window. Toys and sunshine, an expanse of polished floor. The front door is open, warm air blows through; you sit on the front step, waiting. Overhead, a name written in cumulus changes too quickly to read.

෴

A page folded over; a book's spine broken; a word passed hand to hand, secretly. Your head is a file stuffed with pink slips and sticky-notes. Time whines in your ears. In the early dark you go down to the river, that darker panel of water, gliding. Cold narcosis, bed upon bed of black blooms.

You listen for an echo, word-fall, steps in the next room. The head is a bonehouse, pain rising. That thread of yearning sewn in the skin— needles, fire— winter's cusp. A season of mirrors, all your letters running backward to bliss. *I cannot write*, you write— the page explodes. Flaming handfuls of copper, green iris. The glass is thin, so thin.

❧

In my father's house are memory rooms, cells smelling of must and honey. Bees drone down the corridors, Mrs. Mouse waves a twiglet broom. That great eye applied to the window, trying to make out the dim objects within— a baby doll, a box of illegible letters? A nest of grass and ribbons? Faltering mnemonics, the heart's not in it— only a few dead leaves.

Into the house of rain I'd take you— *sshh*, no more words. The walls open into doors, thresholds of held breath. Each room holds a bagatelle for your eyes— a ring, a wedding book, a bed. A tabby's passing smile. Come home.

What if? What if? The unsaid aches in the throat. The door gives a little on its hinges and the room is new, whether from sun-shift or influx of time. A feline instant, gold-eyed. Closing.

❧

The night's white fingers tremble. My twin. I wear a snowflake mantilla, spider's lace. Mistress of thresholds, each room is nested in your breast. No more pain, only the papery folding of black swans. One step— the path closes. Begin again, chasing a leaf of blowing snow.

A house is never safe. Muffled bells, an avalanche warning, doors burst open one by one. The dead are buried in cotton-lined matchboxes— sparrows and moles and baby squirrels, broken. Goldfish frozen in spheres of ice. Purple quartz, the radio blues— *how much, how much can we bear?*

A castle of days is slowly built, block by melting block. Dim interior, white roses in the vestibule. Shelves upon shelves of empty sentences, I no longer want to read them all. Only vowels, letters of snow.

❧

Fair skies. The windows are daubed with petals and questions. A breeze blows through, the house shifts with a sigh. Water prisms— wet rose for passion, blue hyacinth. Exhausted sleep.

We dream larval dreams, wings sheathed. Out— something is breaking out. Here a kiss is lethal. Here the air weeps silk. In sea-cloud she rises, a city of jasper shining in her eye. Hyaline, thin lens between death and imagining.

And always retreating, that light. In my father's house are rainy windows, walls of rainbow facets. Like a latch rusted shut, I would open. Like the cats in the garden, I would spring. Something stirs behind the wall, small hands, nose and mouth pressing in. A child's white dreams, a heap of headless dolls.

❧

Would I prune back the overgrowth of yearning?
Robert Duncan, "Circulations of the Song"

A garden's architecture, sun and moving blocks of cloud.
Rain weeps and spits into leaf-fold, chlorophyll funnels...
thought's run-off. Memory glistens. A spider spins green
intervals, a grid of raindrops, brimming eyes. In rumours
of water, the first ferns of spring. Iris, my lover's spear.
Yearning grows crazed, twining the vertical. Blind animals
in the underbrush, salmonberry, salaal.

Cut back that magnolia's lascivious tongues! Light-pressed,
pink buds on our eyes. Purple crocus of destitution, the wet
earth warming, swelling. Liquid birds. A house of shifting
weathers, garden of gusts and sudden chimes. Cat prints
lead back into mind, into a dim room under cedar-soaked
eaves, the gutters sobbing, choked with leaves. Home—

❧

In memory of Anne Szumigalski

Into the house of snow I'd take you. The coffin is a lonely
bath— foam and twigs, a handful of seeds. Spring green.
Where is the woman with anemones for hair, earth rolls
bolstering her body? Eyes open, marbled, ivy twining the
wrists. We read from lists of sorrows: rose glass, green leaf.
Blue syllables.

Silence, then storm. Angels hiss through the clouds—
stones, stones. There's a trick in spring, sudden dip and
the sky riots, electric. Where is the woman with tentacles
for hair, lightning sheathing her body? We must hide in
the cellar among sacks of tubers, jars of fleshy plums.
Plunging barometers, the radio at four. A cello takes our
hearts.

Scrolls of cloud loom inkier by the minute. A volume
slams shut. New aspens shiver, it's April, May— then June
arrives wreathed with green worms. Where is the woman
with lilacs for breasts, robins tugging at her toes? The
house painters drop their ladders and flee, hail following.
Morning leans in an open door, the air's cool liquor
flowing in.

Moment

St. Peter's Abbey

I would delay the first stroke—
                        but here the moment
breaks
            on its own urgency—
                            full

then empty— save a line of hours
neatly tolled

the first stroke, first moment
                            missed—
still resonant

a hand gathering the air.

A story knelled of death and rain,
wet lilies in her arms

rain on our skins, a lust—

I would delay the sense, but in the holding
lose it
            one drop, another, sliding down the glass
                    her earth-stained face

wind gusting over graves and peonies

our black-shrouded hours—
            crows, yellow leaves
    in June
                oh, hold—
                        a stroke past solstice,
slipping—

Requiem for Spring

> *No, it is not I, it is someone else*
> *who suffers.*
>
> Anna Akhmatova, "Requiem"

1

Kleine Nacht, Celan prays, *take me*
inside. Even as spring's green commas,
licked grasstips. Take me—

take *her,* the other who mourns
in my skin. I am rather inclined to silence.

Not I, but she trembling in me. Lord,
what hope for small things—

baby teeth, a wedding ring.
My silent guitar.

Not I, but another covered
with bitter ash, a lenten renunciation

of wine and sugar. Take her, *take me*
up there, where April stars,

pursed and chaste among bare lilacs—
where the dew pools

into tears. Sshh, a child is crying
as rain pours and rain pours,

drainspouts frothing, chuckling
in the dark.

2

Sweet clover, fistful of childish ferns.
The sun's a wild daisy, the sky
drops
      forget-me-nots—

forget me. It is someone else who leans
into sorrow, auras for quivering leaves.

A land in twilight, sloughs of salty tears.
I can almost see again.

A woman comes veiled in grey, a woman
flying, flying into fire.

I give it up— the grief, its burning wings.
I am scrubbed and sober as a bug.

Spring buds in its cups, shrugs off
the unlovely. Even the sparrow

is gilded, the stray tom fêted
like a prince. If not for dreams

of coming floods, a woman
waking—

3

Gillyflower, pink, the clove of love.
A garden ripens, a muskier air.

Lethe bears the lengthening years, a wake
of dandelions, paper sails.

She, enfolded in the fireflies' blessed script.

It is someone else whose wings, bruised knuckles
batter the glass.

Surrender the line, leafing, opening small mouths.
Surrender the ear's green corolla.

The old world slips and spills,
lily of the valley lingers
                              oh, once

I was a child—
a garden in my arms—

What Remains

The story may well lie there in a cloud.
Michael Palmer, "First Figure"

1

Showers of gold rain— ribbons, wings—
the sun-streaked gods in their bliss

      the heavens a panoply of absence, or rather
absence assuming form,
as if
      feathers, fins, scales, antlers
whiskers   quicksilver jitters—
           the merest—

The story may well lie there in a cloud   or wander
distant airplane glimpsed,

lost—
      an inkling, tail of ice,
frisson—
      who would think, along lines of sunlit aspen,
sky thunder-grey and breaking—

      signs from the north, green ice
          starred calculus— junctures—

Beware, draw back—
      the story may well lie   a lullaby

white tales, the provenance of clouds

2

A sonnet of cut glass, a couplet
of polished jars—

jars upon jars of hard cravings— licorice
kisses, lemon suckers. Words soften

on a sugary tongue. Grenadine, blue mould
on the raspberries, peach.

Sated, sticky with glistening nouns,
sentence after sentence

of vacant promise— writing,
I absorb the ink's bitter scent, circle with white

what's beyond the pen, beyond the words
that blur leftward,

little flurries. A sleepy coupling— feathers,
pillows, twisted sheets, all is not well

with the weather, the moon's cold limbs
ripple over us.

I might have written more.

Rime in my eyes— ice asterisks—

3

Smoke-furred, furious— hissing cats—
flames scour the upper rooms—

           red angels in mine,
tarred parchment in yours—

we are charred, we are flaking, our black-inked kisses
spit— prayers in the intervals
                bless me, burn—
smoky lips brush your face.

           All the clocks in the house expire
one by one— cymbals, *bong—*
                    our grandfathers, ghosts
in heaven, hear the *tock tock tock* of eternal grief—
fires sunder us
           God is at home—
we are in a far country,
burning

no ash, no bone

what words
remain—

Ashes

A library given to fire— the mind's heat, pages curling under blackened thumbs. Reading, my eyes water and smart. Reading, I am reduced to a wisp of smoke, a cone of sandalwood ash. Cockroaches rise from the embers, their insect armour melting to crazy glass. Reading, I am a mouth, a face burned away. I am molten—

incendiary words. Alice and the fat duchess, cook's head in the fire, sparks of hot pepper and screams. Pages caught on a burning sleeve of air. I'm in a furnace and they think I'm reading, a purring cat on my knees.

෴

In dreams I am sleepless and write to fill the hours. I write to fill this white room with paper, reams upon reams. Locked in the room without a pen, I make do with a sooty finger or open a vein. From time to time the door creaks and pages of my life are removed in armloads, baskets, wheelbarrows of ashen words.

When the white room is filled, when I am blackened with
fire and my veins have run dry, I will marry the king who
reads my life. In the long white nights he will disappear
into me, smoothing the vellum, as *if*. A story's dark face,
a moon abducted in a silver wheelbarrow.

ॐ

We are haunted by pages we've never read, pages shelved
too high to read, slipped into scrapbooks among rose petals,
locks of baby hair. Pages of flower sutras, recipes for
poisoned wine. Secret letters folded between "erotica"
and "errata," tucked into tea-stained books: *Sonnets to
Morphia. Narcotic Rhymes. The Book of Dissolving;
The Book of Washing Away. A Child's Book of Clouds* —
locked diaries, whose keys —

Tell me—

1

We wake in sticky heat, the house holding its breath—
red salamanders in the night
                    red fetuses—

the fat dew of morning taken back
with a hiss
            tell me—

when burned trees cleave

when fire is given, taken away then
given again to burn—

when, scraped and flamed, words of polished malachite
        green butterflies—

when the past untwists, a charred strip
and telling is untelling
                    stories taken back
into their own gaps—

We wake into fear, a scene
of ravelling
            damp hair, bedclothes— secrets—

2

Smoke-veiled— the day silted with details,
layers of mind that won't wash clear

      a muddle of errands— newspaper,
cat food, rolls of film—
          all our paths loopy, hopeless,
homebound—
      stations of the daily cross—

convulsive neurotransmitters, rivers
of dim nerves—

Well, the only clarity is in whisky and ice,
the day now amber, suspended—

      you try to ride a bubble of thought
          until it bursts— yes!

just a minute—

      shit, the smoke from the north
is getting denser by the hour
          the children coughing,
colds thickening and you mired
in yearning

      even a dose of daily reality—
a little medicinal neural rearrangement—

will never cure you.

Sheol

Broken sleep— light, the sea
flooding in
                I had thought to write for relief—
but tortured by light, the sea
flooding in—
          ssshhh,
try to sleep —

Ugly fish nudge the kitchen window,
dogfish, puffers
            electric eels—

Could I hide in the sanctity of my suffering,
could I burrow to Sheol and beyond—

       not Caliban in his pinched afflictions,
kittens fallen into rusty wells—

       I have seen the small slack offspring of lust,
indifference
          listen— *it's the sea in your ear*

a lullaby
       no sleep— please—

Breaking the Lines

The imperfect is our paradise.
Note that, in this bitterness, delight,
Since the imperfect is so hot in us,
Lies in flawed words and stubborn sounds.
              Wallace Stevens, "The Poems of Our Climate"

I am dreaming awake, waking
from a long dream of burial,
the earth-mound shuddering, heaving
beneath me. I am breaking the lines
with terrible care, as if to write
were to kneel on groaning ice—
sprays of brittle stars—
those far white fires above us
vanishing. Cold ashes, vice,
the imperfect is our paradise.

Glass solstice mansions—
manic visions of fire, whores,
hooded heads with glittering
pierced lips— one kiss, as if
to write were to taste
a subtle poison. Bitter white
precipitate of aspirin hours, of tea
and deciphering the starry page.
To hold, then relinquish— write—
note that, in this bitterness, delight.

Stone lion-heads under caps of snow,
migraines, the glittering script
of getting through—X-
rayed limbs, cold fetishes. Words,
erased, insist on the nerve, as if
to write were to enter loss—
an errancy, light failing us.
We dream by the fire with Yeats
and Poe, black stars to dust,
the imperfect is so hot in us.

Of winter thorns, thought's circling
returns. A peregrine in hand,
a bush of screaming beaks.
The cat skitters in. I am tracing
the unbending weather, as if to write
were to take the outmost route around
the hour— call for more wine,
close your eyes in the dusk.
Eclipsed. Our bliss, our wounds
lie in flawed words and stubborn sounds.

Nerves, I am

Do the dead rumble beneath everything?
Annie Dillard, *For the Time Being*

1

Sweet fungus, mango,
orange peel—
         some spongy matter
at the base of the brain—
lust runs filaments
                  through the dark

wet asphalt
         a woman's body below,
the whole world an ache,
so that—
         new teeth on edge,
gums nubbed, raw with want—

Our days invert
and vanish, little licks
of glitter, skin—
                  whose eyes
see the question dimpling
below?
         blinds wink
and laughter— TV flicker
dims the system—

             put your ear
to my breast, tickle switches
up the ribs—
             oh you
are my underside— wet leaves
your words
             smell, allow
cool

blue as corruption.

2

How the bones roll—
how the heavy ash of unbeing drifts
over lifted faces—
             do the dead rumble,
do they growl in their sleep?

A bass, subterranean thunder
wakes us
          fire of copper, azure
                        lucifers
a continuous deep
pavane

          nerves, I am
earth under earth, ambiguous
cessation
          bees, bees,
silence, whispers

dark's death-mask, a profile
of sunless days

          veins of mercury, iron

                    I am
slow, I am old,
a big old cat mouldering
into sleep
            listen—
                    that elegy
in the leaves   a breeze

or mice— nerves—
            or less, or less

        an eyelash—

                    light
assenting

Debris

1

Horned husk— *scratchscratch*—
I must, I *must*—
        winter leaves
rasped away, the skin
in lucid shreds
        scab, bract—

first perception, insight
in blunt nubs—
        raw, the flesh turns,
flash of fish scales
on inner wrist, iridescence
on lip and gill

        and stripped to the pores—
rind and fibre, the very oil
of longing—
        orange blossom,
citrus peel,
curls of arbutus,
rotting fruit, debris—
        faint foamline on our thighs.

Come in, the lamp is lit,
its long wick dipped in honey, amber
        words flicker, wink
on the page—
        oh, I could read all summer and into
the dark, sheer flames appearing
on my body.

2

Dying again in Venice,
Paris
  and the Vancouver night
smelling of sake, fish
and danger—
    fingertips,
our tongues in the dark
warm, lapping—

   afloat with stars
on the milky sea,
our bodies buoyed—
    lifted—

the cities below
  phosphorescent.

In the morning,
water quiet in the sun, we recover
kelp outlines—
   my hand, your ear, a curl of hair—
    faint oil sheen

an arbutus drops
its skin.

Autumn Soup

The gardener's cat is dead, the gardener gone
And last year's garden grows salacious weeds.
Wallace Stevens, "Credences of Summer"

The gardener's cat is dead, the gardener gone.
The gate swings open in the thickening dusk
and last year's garden grows salacious weeds.
I am sinking to the bottom, storm-green.

The gate swings open in the thickening dusk.
A ghost cat preens and glimmers in the glass.
I am sinking to the bottom, storm-green,
the colour of bracken, steeped leaves.

A ghost cat preens and glimmers in the glass.
Squat on the stove, a pot of autumn soup
the colour of bracken, steeped leaves.
It's late, the dead fly in with the dark.

Squat on the stove, a pot of autumn soup;
a kettle of crabs clacks and boils.
It's late, the dead fly in with the dark.
Storm cloud, rosy claw over the sea.

A kettle of crabs clacks and boils—
I've lost appetite, nerve, my impetuous flesh.
Storm cloud, rosy claw over the sea,
it all washes up in our soft, hollowed bed.

I've lost appetite, nerve, my impetuous flesh.
Listen to the water, briny tide of years—
it all washes up in our soft, hollowed bed,
in sleep, night's weeds twisting over us.

Through the Galleries

Gabriola Island, B.C.

Sleep is all— words calcified into shell, ink-specked. My
hand reads the braille. The object of desire is at the bottom
of a tidal pool. The eye's hunger for subtle colours— oyster,
crab— tints of tumbled shells, cloudy beach. Sea recedes,
a veil of foam flecking our skin. At one end, the island is
polished smooth; the other end is pocked with craters.
Thought wears down in nubs and wavy layers. The perfect
shell is under here— no there, between two rocks, there,
a hermit vision.

Waves erode the heart, remould. Salt-spray, the day served
out in cups. Stone toadstools pocked with finger-sized holes.
Water flows over. Water flows over. White ferry on the
horizon, beyond the farthest swimmers. Come and eat a
doll's picnic of clams and sea-lettuce, egg-white pebbles.
My swimsuit's worn thin, I'll leave it to bleach on that log.
I meet my footprints coming and going. The best route is
through the sandstone galleries— always round the next
bend, the next—

Glosses and Tongues

Were there moon—
 were there mind, new light
through blinds, a louvred play
of lived—
 unlived—

the heart sliced into beautiful slides,
stained carmine
 what eye, unblinking,
gazing—

moments tilted in the light,
turned over—
 the night face of being—

I'd see it climb its marble stairs—
moon of metaphor, veiled
 for the bridal

෪

A little rain, summer river
whose skin—
 black rivulets, clouds
electric—

on waterfilm, I'd see the minutes running backward,
rain returning to cloud.

Dark winds consume one elm after another
a moment's ash or fiery verso

and wings pack the sandbars, listen—
faint, a rumour of drinking and water.

The years enter like thieves
stay awake—

quick secretive kneeling mists,
prayers like grey gloves.

In waves, in waves we drift out
to the islands
the moon of *what if* ascending the sky

our minds like logs on a swell—
rolling under

purple stars *in the scalloped edgewaters*

blue heron, quite still.

Notes

Chang Heng's "The Bones of Chuang Tzu," from which the epigraph to "Nine Wilds" is taken, can be found in the *Anthology of Chinese Literature: From Early Times to the Fourteenth Century*, ed. Cyril Birch (Grove Press, 1965).

In "To the Bonehouse," the term *"cadavre exquis"* is taken from the essay, "Maladie du deuil et fantasme du cadavre exquis" by Maria Torok, a French psychoanalyst; the essay can be found in Torok and Nicolas Abraham, *L'Écorce et le noyau* (Flammarion, 1987).

"Nature morte" is based on Paul Cézanne's painting "Still Life with Flowers in an Olive Jar."

"The Book of Spleen" Part 1 is based on Michael Palmer's poem "Autobiography 2 (hellogoodby)" in *The Promises of Glass* (New Directions, 2000).

The epigraph to "Woman Reading 1" is from Michael Palmer's "On the Way to Language" in his *The Lion Bridge: Selected Poems, 1972-1995* (New Directions, 1998).

"Woman Reading 2" is based on Édouard Vuillard's painting "Woman Reading" (1896).

"Woman in a Striped Dress" is based on Édouard Vuillard's painting of the same title (1895).

The epigraph to "Digression" is from Susan Howe's "Pythagorean Silence" in her book of the same title (Montemora Foundation, 1982).

The epigraph to "Weather Notes: St. Peter's Abbey" is from Fred Wah's "Father/Mother Haibun #3," one of a sequence of haibun in *Waiting for Saskatchewan* (Turnstone, 1985).

The italicised phrases in "Dwelling," p.46, are from Wallace Stevens's "Variations on a Summer Day" in *The Collected Poems of Wallace Stevens* (Vintage, 1982).

The epigraph to "Dwelling," p.59, is from Robert Duncan's "Circulations of the Song" in *Ground Work: Before the War* (New Directions, 1984).

The italicised phrases in "Requiem for Spring" are from Paul Celan's "Little Night" ("Kleine Nacht"), trans. Michael Hamburger, in *Selected Poems* (Penguin, 1996).

The italicised material in "What Remains" (1) is from Michael Palmer's "First Figure," which can be found in *The Lion Bridge*.

"God is at home, we are in a far country" is from Meister Eckhart, cited by Annie Dillard in *Holy the Firm* (Harper & Row, 1977).

The italicised phrases in "Glosses and Tongues" are from Jorie Graham's "Emergency" in *The Errancy* (Ecco, 1997).

Acknowledgements

Until her death in the spring of 1999, Anne Szumigalski lent her ear to many of these poems, as did Elizabeth Brewster, Tonja Gunvaldsen Klaassen, Elyse Yates St. George, and the others in our Saskatoon poetry group. Thank you also for feedback from Don McKay and the poetry "colloquistas" at the Sage Hill Writing Experience (Summer 1998). As well, I was very fortunate to have Tim Lilburn's feedback at a crucial point, when the manuscript was beginning to gel, again at Sage Hill (Fall 2000).

*H*ilary Clark lives in Saskatoon, where she teaches English and Women's & Gender Studies at the University of Saskatchewan. She has published an earlier book, *More Light*, with Brick (1998), and another book of poems, *Two Heavens*, with Hagios Press (1998). In 1999, *More Light* was awarded the Pat Lowther Memorial Award and the Saskatchewan Book Award for Poetry.